Live your

`D1507131`

Intention!

Be Inspird

Septembr 30, 2020

Danielle Butt

" Yoga for a Cause "

Your Life.

Your Career.

Your Choice!

A True Story of Achievement
Against the Odds

Danielle Brit

ISBN: 9798654030726
Imprint: Independently published

Table of Contents

"Make a pact with yourself now:
to not be defined by your past.
The greatest benefit of hard work is not
what you get. It's what you become."

Introduction

Dear friend,

Your Life. Your Career. Your Choice! is a professional development book based on a true story...

... *my* story.

I was raised in a poor family, lived in a trailer park, and struggled day in and day out. Still, I had a dream of one day becoming a successful businesswoman. I maintained that dream through extremely challenging circumstances: enduring the trauma of sexual abuse as a child, being homeless, losing several family members, divorce, and more. Yet, despite all the many trials I have experienced: I persevered beyond those limitations. This is the message I want to get across to anyone who is searching for deeper meaning in his or her life.

After reading *Your Life. Your Career. Your Choice!* it is my whole-hearted desire that, as a result of my story, you will gain insights you can use for your professional and personal development. Firstly, I hope you'll feel inspired, grateful, and appreciative for wherever you are in your life right now. Secondly, I wish to encourage you to take the next step: set new goals, make your plan, take action, and reach your dreams while never allowing anyone or anything to stop you.

Hard work, dedication, and fortitude are the top qualities you need to become anything you want in your life.

Enjoy the book.

Danielle Britt

Chapter One:

Bewilderment Meets Success

"There has to be more

to life than this."

Standing in the living room of our white two-story house, I looked through the front screen door and admired one of the tall trees growing along-side the riverbank. I could see our freshly cut grass, the two-lane road at the end of the lawn, and the river on the other side of the street. I could hardly believe where we were.

That home represented a significant milestone for my family. We grew up poor. Most everything we ate was either grown in our garden or an animal we hunted. I went hunting and fishing with my father as often as he would let me. I also worked on our one-acre garden daily.

I would plant, till the soil, water the seeds, and even spread horse manure as fertilizer! There were times my parents sent me to collect the wild blackberries that grew near our garden. We filled up the truck bed with our home-grown vegetables, my little baskets full of blackberries, and drove to a busy road that had a wide dirt shoulder. We parked on the side of the road, and sold our vegetables to the people who passed by.

There were also many times my mom dropped us off at a community garbage dumpster behind one of the local retail stores. My brothers and I would go dumpster diving, searching for clothes or shoes we could use. If the clothing was wearable, we used it. Other times, we would mend the articles and exchange them for money, or something that would fit.

Whenever we were driving with my mom, if we passed an aluminum can, she would stop the car and tell one of us kids to collect it. We'd jump back in the car and take off. If someone happened to be driving by, I can't tell you how embarrassing I felt, having them see me step out and pick those cans up.

One time, my parents sent us to work for a man, picking green beans. The man paid my parents $5 for a 5-gallon bucket full of beans. My little fingers were blistered and torn up after those work sessions. But we needed the money, and my parents found any way we could to make it. No complaining.

We were on Medicaid and food stamps. My dad worked multiple odd jobs. Sometimes he was a mechanic. Other times he was a landscaper, a painter, or basically anything he could to make money. People came in and out of our house frequently. My father was constantly changing someone's oil or fixing a random repair for less money than one of the local mechanics would. He always started his day with a cup of coffee and ended it with beer; as many beers as he could afford to drink.

We had lived in a run-down trailer, in a run-down trailer park. At night, when I'd walk through the doorway into the kitchen, I closed my eyes and vibrated with fear. There was no point trying to avoid it, though: as soon as I turned the light on, a party of roaches scurried all over the floor and walls to escape into whichever of the many cracks they could find. I still cringe at the thought of those little creeps.

Standing in the doorway of our new home, those memories were finally part of the past. I was looking across the road at the trees blowing in the wind, thinking about where we had come from. Those countless side-of-the-road garden sales, dumpster dives, bags full of aluminum cans, and all sorts of odd jobs; our family was finally able to move into that two-story white house and start a new life.

In order to afford our new home, my father was working harder than ever. We were still renting. Yet, we were moving up. My father took pride in that. We all did. My mother was taking care of us and kept the house clean and organized. Our life probably appeared normal from the outside looking in. Yet, moving to a new environment doesn't necessarily mean things are improving. My mother frequently accused my dad of cheating on her. My parents fought a lot. Their fighting often became physical.

One night, my father hit my mother over the head with a beer bottle, smashing it into pieces while screaming at her. Our neighbors called the police and an ambulance. My mother had to go to the hospital to get one-hundred and eighteen stitches. The police did not let us go back home. We ended up staying in a safe house for a week or so. That was pretty common. She never pressed charges. The situation would just cool down after a while. Then, it would start again another time. Most nights usually ended with them fighting and screaming. Physical abuse became a habit between both of them. In the morning, my mother often had new bruises all over her body. I always asked her to leave my dad, but she wouldn't. She stayed and kept allowing the mayhem to continue. She believed in her vows: *for better or for worse*.

I have two brothers. I am the middle child. My youngest brother is my father's favorite, and the oldest is my mother's. I was the one left in the blind-spot; often left out of regular family outings. That's not self-pity. It's just a fact. I often found myself day-dreaming, thinking of what a better life could look like. I remember thinking to myself: "There has to be more to life than this."

On this particular day, while I stood in the doorway looking at the front yard, something became crystal clear in my imagination. It was an image that entered my mind. It was a vision of the future. I said the words under my breath and heard them loudly in my mind: "I will be successful one day." Then, I envisioned myself being an adult, dressed in a business suit, standing in a tall building, looking out over a city. I heard the words: "New York." At that moment, I saw the life I was going to pursue. It would be dramatically different from the life our family was living.

I was tired of hearing my parents argue about money. The feelings were exacerbated by going to school and standing in the line for free breakfast and lunch. I envied the kids who brought their lunch boxes. Now, looking back, I'm thankful to have been raised in a country that could support those free lunches. Yet, at that point in time, all I could think about was how those kids must have had money if they could afford bringing food to school in a lunch box. I hated not having money for ice cream at snack time. A wonderful and kind girl shared her snacks with me on our bus ride home, though. I thought to myself: "One day I want to be able to buy someone else snacks, too."

I felt embarrassed that we had to get clothes and shoes during Christmas from the Salvation Army Angel Tree. I was ashamed that my basketball shoes had holes in them. Rainy days equaled wet feet. I wanted to be successful so bad. I didn't want anyone to provide for me. All I had were those experiences, and those feelings to use as raw material. I had a vision. I had a dream. My situation created that vision that got locked into my mind. I started striving from that day forward.

Have you ever thought to yourself: *there has to be more to life than this?*

Have you ever pictured what your future could become?

Have you ever wondered, if you *really* went for the "next level," what you could accomplish?

You may feel like you're in a rut. Perhaps it has been a while and you feel like you're growing complacent. Circumstances are not working in your favor and you can't see a way out. You may feel stagnant, locked into the situation you're in, living paycheck to paycheck, or wondering to yourself: "Is this the life I'm destined to have?"

I understand how you feel. Sometimes, from that perspective, it's like there is no solution. However, there most certainly is a solution. The good news is this: you can get out of any rut and turn your situation around. Those stagnant and stuck perspectives, a complacent mindset – they can all change with one little choice.

It's just a subtle mindset shift.

It's a spark, when you say to yourself: "I have had enough."

That spark ignites a new flame.

Of course, anything worthwhile takes time, energy, and effort. You're reading this book right now. That is a positive action toward your new future. That is something to be proud of. You are currently, in this very moment, investing in yourself. That shows you are capable of achieving something new in your life.

For me, while standing in that doorway, my mind drifting to the image of a skyscraper and business suit in New York, I knew there had to be more to life than everything appearing perfect on the outside, yet falling apart on the inside.

In 1956, a man named Earl Nightingale produced an album called *The Strangest Secret.* It sold over a million copies, which made it the first Gold *spoken-word* recording! In that album, Earl defines success as: "The progressive realization of a worthy ideal." I love that definition. Specifically, I love the word *progressive.* It's not a result. It's not an event. It's something that continually progresses and unfolds as time goes on. You are, right now, on a progression. In order to apply that principle to your life, it is important to define what your *next* progression looks and feels like. In other words, what do you really want?

Take out a notebook and begin writing some of your dreams and goals.

For example:

- I want to learn Spanish
- I want to become a welder
- I want to have children
- I want a new truck
- I want to play golf
- I want to complete High School
- I want to be a millionaire
- I want to lose 20 lbs.
- I want to be happy
- I want to be a better person
- I want to be optimistic

Write down anything, and everything you want. Just allow your mind to go free. Then, for any one of those desires, chunk it down into something more specific. For instance, when do you want to accomplish that by? One year? Two? Three years?

Next, what are you going to *do* to get there? What's your action plan? What's the next step? Take some form of action, right now. Make the call. Invest in the course. Tell someone you respect. Take action. Let me give you some examples of what that may look like…

- I want to learn Spanish: I am going to study for 3o minutes a day and find a Spanish teacher first thing tomorrow morning.
- I want to have children: Is my partner the person I really want to have kids with? How much money do I need to raise a child? Do I want to be married first? Should I create better living conditions?
- I want to become a welder: I'm going to ask the guidance counselor how to become a welder and follow that process.
- I want a new truck: Find out how much a new truck will cost, what kind of job should I get to afford that, and how much should I start saving.
- I want to play a better game of golf: I am going to the driving range, or golf course two days each week.

- I want to be a millionaire: Review my financial statements next week with my accountant, schedule a meeting with someone who is a millionaire, and ask them what they did. Create a better financial plan.
- I want to lose 20 Lbs.: I will drink water, instead of sugary beverages. I'll stop eating sugar for the next ten days, and then I will treat myself to a beverage and dessert of my choice.
- I want to be happy and more optimistic: I will wake up fifteen minutes earlier each day to listen to a motivational speaker, and whenever negative thoughts pop into my head I will refocus on what I'm grateful and appreciative for.

Asking for what you want is the first step.

Defining the next action: that's the second step.

The third, fourth, fifth, and every step after that is: *action, action, and more action*.

Chapter Two:

Taking Out Head Trash

*"The words you speak have power
to the degree of your inner voice."*

At thirteen years old, I was over at a friend's house and we checked the mail before heading to basketball practice. A lady approached in her car and invited us to a revival they were having at church the following night. She said, "There will be cute boys there." Suddenly, it sounded like quite an interesting event. The next night, we attend the church service. There were a bunch of absolutely beautiful cars in the parking lot. One of the cars was a BMW. I fell in love with that car. As we walked in, we were greeted with many smiling friendly faces. Almost everyone there was dressed in a suit, or a beautiful gown. I enjoyed the church service. It felt peaceful, and much different than what my life was like at home. I continued going to church after that night. I started getting invited to lunches, and ate with all sorts of different people after the service. The youth leaders really seem to like me. They invited me over to their homes. The first time I went to one of their houses I remember noticing how clean it was. It smelled so good. They had several vehicles and even a car phone! I knew those were the type of people I wanted to surround myself with. I thought to myself, "Maybe they can help me figure out how to get a real job and not be poor like my family." I realized I was surrounding myself with people who were doing better than my parents in more areas of life than just money. They spoke clearer, and had real discussions with one another, and worked out challenges as a family. They did not throw things at each other, scream, or hit one another. I loved the examples they set forth. It kept me going to church.

My mother often grounded me from church. She knew I loved going there, and she usually punished me by keeping me from going to events I liked. One night I was supposed to be in bed, but I heard my parents fighting again, so I snuck down the stairs just enough to peek around the corner. I saw my mom sitting on the couch. My dad was sitting in his chair beside the coal stove. The TV was on, playing the news. I listened closely. I heard my mom accusing my dad of not working that day. She said, "So, where did you work today? Did you go see your girlfriend?"

My dad replied, "I don't have a girlfriend."

She said, "What did you do all day, then?"

He said, "I worked, damnit. I worked. What did you do all day? Sit on your ass?"

She said, "I cleaned this house and I cooked dinner. Dinner that you didn't eat because you were with your girlfriend."

My dad replied, "I was working, damnit."

My mom said "How much money did you make today?"

My dad reached in his back pocket and grabbed his brown leather wallet. He opened it and showed my mom the money inside. My mom then said "How much is that?" My dad replied "I don't know. Enough." My mom said, "Let me see your wallet." my dad threw it hard at her face. She jumped up and started cussing at him. My dad stood up, picked up the chair he was sitting on and hit my mom with it repeatedly. I started shaking and crying, ran back up the stairs, and snuck back into bed. I thought "My dad is going to kill her one day." I laid in bed and I knew the next day would be full of tension.

I woke up the next morning and had a lot on my mind. Not only the fight that happened the night before, but I had been holding onto something secret that I felt ashamed of. I couldn't tell anyone about this situation. It was becoming more painful as the days went on. A close family member had been sexually abusing me. For the purpose of this book, I will keep this individual's identity private. I will also not share the specific details. However, the situation was real, and it was eating at my soul. I had kept it a secret for too long. I assumed if I told my parents, they would think I was lying and if any of us kids were caught lying, we'd get the switch. In this situation it was true: a person was taking advantage of me, and I was suffering constantly. I didn't know what to do. So, I just kept everything hidden. It was the easiest way to avoid being accused of lying, and getting bruises and welts on my butt and legs from the switch.

I wanted to tell my mom about this individual who was hurting me because I wanted the abuse to stop. I had so many thoughts about how my parents wouldn't believe me, even if I told them.

When I woke up that day, I decided I was going to tell my mother what had been happening. Enough was enough. This had to stop. I planned on going fishing early in the day, and committed to telling her when I arrived back home. I grabbed my fishing pole and walked to the river. I loved sitting by the side and watching the water flow passed. It was so peaceful and quiet. The sounds of nature were beautiful. No one was fighting or arguing. It was my escape from all the tension and drama.

I heard my brothers approaching in the background. They were walking toward the river bank. I took a deep breath in and thought to myself "I just want to be alone. Please go away." As soon as they started walking down the hill, my youngest brother said to me, "Did you break my fishing pole?" I said "No." He said, "Well, I didn't break it and I know our brother didn't break it. So, it had to be you." I replied, "I swear, I didn't break it. I've been using this green one." My oldest brother stood there listening. He didn't really say much. He just laughed a little. My youngest brother said, "Well, I'm telling mom and dad you broke it." It was turning into the absolute worst day. I held in my tears until my brothers left. That morning I had woken up feeling as sad as a human could feel, and desperately needed to get my secret off my chest. Mom and dad had a big fight the night before. I thought, "Now, I'm going to get a whipping for something I didn't do." I felt helpless, sitting on the river bank. I stayed for another hour or so. I headed back up to the house.

When I arrived back, my dad confronted me about the fishing pole. I pleaded that I didn't do it, but my brother had convinced him. He said, "Go pick out your switch." I got whipped with the switch and the belt. I went to my room and sat on my bed, looking at the welts on my butt and legs. When I came out of my room, I saw my mother sitting on the porch. I walked through the door and sat down beside her on the step. We began talking about various things. I kept thinking about the conversation I wanted to bring up. I was nervous. I was afraid she wouldn't believe me. I was trying to get the head trash out of my thoughts. I finally got the courage to say, "Mom, I need to tell you something." She looked at me. "I am being touched by x." She replied, "Seriously, Danielle? That is not true. Why are you telling these things to me?"

I was devastated.

I thought she may not believe me, yet I was crushed, nonetheless. The knot in my throat kept twisting into bunches. I felt nothing and everything at the same time. The tears started building up. "I am not lying. It has happened more than once. I have been holding this in for weeks. I just wanted to tell you and get this off of my chest." She sat and looked into the distance as if she didn't want to acknowledge me in any way. I don't know if she didn't believe me, or if she did but wouldn't face the truth. It didn't matter. I got up and walked to my room. So tired of being left at home, left out, and ignored. I was angry at being grounded from the only thing that made me happy: church. I was exhausted from being accused of lying, and whipped for it. I wanted so badly for that conversation to provide comfort. I felt used, unwanted, and unloved.

Later that night, everyone was sitting in the living room watching Saturday Night Live and eating catfish. I kept my distance. I tried to make myself as small and invisible as possible. The house was warm and smelled like burning coal from our fireplace. Some of the catfish, I had personally caught. I felt pretty happy about that. Then, sitting there eating quietly, I started hearing the head trash: "You're not wanted. You're not desired. You're not loved. They don't believe you. You're better off dead than alive." I kept repeating these words to myself. I gazed through the TV. I couldn't hear anything in the room. I wasn't focused on anything other than those words.

My youngest brother said something. Everyone was looking at me. I said, "What?" He said, "That's how you probably broke the fishing pole."

I replied, "I did not break the fishing pole, and I already got whipped for it. Can we just drop this?"

He said, "But I know you did it."

I stood up, got off the couch, and said, "No. I didn't. I am so sick and tired of being accused of doing things I haven't done. You two never get in trouble." (Pointing at my brothers) and then I looked at my mom and said, "You don't believe me either and I came to you in private to tell you about what was happening to me. You don't believe me." Tears built up in my eyes, and I turned and walked back to my room.

The voice came again, and louder this time: "You're not wanted. You're not desired. You're not loved. They don't believe you. You're better off dead than alive." The head trash was building up. It was urging me in the direction of my bedroom, toward my dresser. I walked through my doorway, into my room, and opened the seashell trinket box sitting on the top of the dresser. Inside the box, I had accumulated approximately fifteen Ritalin tablets from the previous two weeks. I had been putting them under my tongue and acting as if I swallowed them. I reasoned that two week's supply would

19

be enough to end my life. I was thirteen and felt there was no purpose in living. I was ready to leave this world. I opened the box and I poured all the pills into my hand. My palm was full. At the lowest, most painful, hollow, and heartbroken moment, I walked out into the living room looking at my parents and brothers and I said "You don't have to worry about believing me anymore more. I will take care of that for you." I then moved my palm toward my mouth and swallowed all of the pills.

When I placed the pills in my mouth, my mom jumps off of the couch screaming and running toward me. My parents both grabbed one of my arms and pulled me into the kitchen. Mom opened the refrigerator and grabbed a pot full of spoiled homemade chicken noodle soup. It was absolutely disgusting. She opened it and forced me to drink it. Before it hit my lips, I could smell the mold. I was gagging at the thought of it. The smell was even worse. I fought back. I screamed, "I just want to die! Leave me alone! I hate feeling like this!" My dad held me down as my mom poured the spoiled soup down my throat. They took me to the bathroom and made me vomit. Then, we went to the hospital. The day ended at some point, thankfully. It was one of the worst. Yet, it did result in a positive shift.

When I arrived back home, it seemed like I had a certain immunity from the family's drama. They left me alone. The person who had been taking advantage of me left me alone as well. I was thankful. The further separation, the better. I wanted to spend more time with the positive influences at church.

That decision at thirteen years-old impacted how I handled rejection throughout the rest of my life. Yes, I learned to keep secrets and protect myself. Yet, I also demonstrated courage in communicating something was wrong, even if I didn't get positive feedback. Courage is something that results in self-esteem.

I also learned that it is not the words you speak out loud that have the most power. It is the voice you repeat to yourself inside your mind that controls you. Every person has that voice in their head, and there are going to be bad days where that voice is saying the most vicious and painful things to you. You are going to feel like staying in bed and being left alone. Going to work will feel like an impossibility. Life, at that moment, may appear purposeless, meaningless, and not worth living. It *is* worth living, however. These experiences are meant to make you stronger. They are meant to make you better. They are like weights in a gym: more pressure equals growth.

Managing your emotions and head trash begins when you guide the thoughts and feelings within yourself. Sometimes the process feels absolutely impossible, I know. Yet, it *is* possible. It is also critical if you want to succeed. When you are not mindful of your emotions, you react automatically. For me, it didn't feel like I had control of my hand that took those pills. However, it *was* my choice. I did have another option. If you don't respond to stressful situations with controlled emotions, you are going to be reactive and out of control.

Let's take a moment to reflect on this:

- Do you ever find yourself feeling like giving up because things don't seem to be going the way you imagined?
- Do you ever want to escape the reality of your circumstances or situations, instead of confronting them head on?
- Do you want to quit and move somewhere far away, expecting things to be different when you get there?

You are not alone if you have had those feelings. They are common and nothing to be ashamed about. Having said that, your feelings are *your* responsibility. You have the power to change them. Actually, *only you* have the power to change them. Never allow people to control your feelings. *Choose* your emotions by directing that inner voice inside your head where you want it to go. You can take your power back and choose how to feel. It is your choice to believe someone else's perceptions. You can allow those perceptions to take control of your mind, or you can direct them where they belong: separate from you, your self-worth, and your self-esteem.

It is your choice how you respond to life's difficult situations. Your outlook on life is a decision away. If you speak negative thoughts to yourself, you're going to believe them at some point. They will become your reality. If you speak positive thoughts to yourself, you may struggle to accept them at first, but eventually you will think positively out of habit. Your thoughts, even in the most horrible situations, will be wired toward solutions and transformation. That does not mean you won't have days where you allow negative thoughts in. Our mind is like a garden, and it is natural to have some weeds that sprout through the ground. When they do pop through, it's up to you, the gardener, to pull them from the root. It is your choice to shut those voices down, and replace them with positive words. Choose to be optimistic. Choose to be happy. Choose to be positive.

Eventually it becomes natural. Remember: your circumstances do not define you!

"If you think negatively, you're going to be negative."

"Your mind and attitude are powerful tools in your life toolbox."

Chapter Three:

Seeds in Adversity

"When life presents you with stumbling blocks, turn them into stepping stones."

At fourteen years-old, I joined a youth group. The group came to Arkansas for a big conference. I was surprised and thankful my parents let me go. After going to the hospital, my parents loosened up on their discipline. I wouldn't say we worked anything out. It was more that everyone just left me alone. I'm thankful that church became my new habit, as opposed to drugs and whichever substances people turn to when encountering similar situations.

I was going to church a lot more. It was becoming like a second home. I was building new relationships with the families there. I felt like I was developing many *second families*, and becoming more conscious about who I was hanging out with. I was focused on surrounding myself with the most successful people in the church. The Pastor, his wife, and the youth leaders were the people I gravitated to most. I learned that they owned their own companies. They wore suits to every service. I chose to surround myself with them as often as I could, hoping their wisdom would catch onto me. They were taking me under their wing. I think they knew things weren't going well at home, and they wanted to share as much wisdom with me as possible. They picked me up for church a lot too.

I am in Arkansas attending the church camp for the week. During camp they have lots of competitions for various sports and may other things. I have been learning that one of the keys to succeeding in life is developing a healthy competitive spirit. There are people who are better at a game, and we can model those people, and also try to win against them. There are people who are just as good as us. We compete with them. There are also people who we are better than. Those are the ones we mentor. The camp was a perfect environment to practice those new insights I was gaining. As a result, I ended up winning "Camper of the Year" with over 1,000 kids in attendance. I also won first place in jump-rope and horseshoe throwing. Those accomplishments felt good. It was so different than my upbringing, constantly ignored and feeling unloved. Before school was let out, I won my first "fastest one-mile race," and was playing on a basketball team too. I was heavily into acrobatics and gymnastics. All the physical activity and competition was a great way to refocus my mind on things I could control. Some people shy away from competitive sports. I think they're critical for building self-esteem, determination, and confidence. Even if you're the worst player on the team. If you change your perspective, and keep your eye on a person who's just a little better than you, and you practice harder, you will notice improvements. At some point, you'll gain positive feedback that your hard work paid off. That feels good, and you become addicted to that feeling.

My parents were arguing less at the time. I think it was due to my mother getting a job as an in-house nurse. She worked with elderly people a few times a week. That got her out of the house and kept her focused on her own priorities, which I'm sure built self-esteem too. I think that also kept her mind off my father's whereabouts. Her job brought in more money, of course, which allowed me to do more things with the church.

Life was taking a new turn.

On the way back from camp, we were travelling from Arkansas and the youth leader's wife asked us girls if we wanted to stay the night with her family instead of going home. The other girls called their parents and they said they could stay. I called my dad and asked if I could stay too. He said yes. Us girls were excited that we got to stay all night. We played games in the car ride back. We were laughing non-stop and having a good time.

When it was time to go to sleep, I slipped into bed and looked at the ceiling for a while. As my eyes grew heavier, I felt a smile on my face. I noticed my body wasn't tense or amped up. My guard was down for the first time, probably in years. I thought to myself: "So, this is what happiness feels like." It was contentment and satisfaction. It was a unique feeling. With that feeling in my heart, I reflected on the youth leaders and their character. I loved being with them. They ate good quality food and prepared it with intention. They were very generous people. They bought me gifts when we went places, and made it their priority that everyone in our group felt included in the activities. They also helped pay for me to go to Arkansas. I could tell, they really loved each other too. They lived clean lifestyles, and never drank or smoked. They never fought. It was such a contrast from my parent's house.

Our personal lives can often feel like "that's how life *is.*" We have a certain perspective. It is what we believe about the world. It's the lens we see life through. It's the only world we know. Yet, when you get around people who are living differently – people who are practicing a higher set of standards than you're used to – their example reveals new possibilities about what you can become. That was the feeling I was soaking into as everything faded and I fell asleep.

The next morning, we woke up and discussed what we were going to do that day. We were going to run to the saw mill to pick up checks so the youth leaders could pay their employees. Then, we were going to get lunch. Then, they were going to take us home. We stopped for lunch at Burger King. It felt special because my family rarely took us out like that, even to a fast-food restaurant like BK. I went to the bathroom. When I came back out, I felt like everyone was acting weird. I'm not a very nosey person, so I didn't ask any questions. I figured if they wanted me to know something, they would tell me. When we left the parking lot, the youth leader said, "Danielle, we are going to your grandmother's house instead of your parent's." I didn't think anything of it, so I said okay. It seemed weird, but not anything to worry about. I was excited to see my mom and show her a bell I bought her in Arkansas. It had a little ice-skater on the side, and I couldn't wait for her to see it. We arrived at my grandmother's. We were walking up the stairs. The girls and the youth leader helped me carry my bags. I had the bell in my hand to give it to my mom. I opened the door and I saw my dad sitting on a chair in front of the kitchen. My grandmother was standing in the kitchen. And my aunt was on the couch. My mom wasn't there. Something wasn't right. A sinking feeling pinpointed my gut, and it grew heavier. I asked, "Where's mom?" My dad walked up to me with tears in his eyes, put his arms around me and said "Your mom died last night." I pushed him back in shock and said "What? How?" My face is swelling red. I could not hold back. The tears were streaming down my cheeks. My dad replied, "It happened last night in her sleep, but we don't know the cause." He explained how she woke up in the middle of the night, gasping for air, looked a little colored, and when he asked her if she was okay, she replied "Yes." I grabbed my dog, Fluffy, and walked to the back bedroom. I didn't know how to feel. Numb. Shocked. Thoughts and feelings of ambiguity. Thoughts ran through my mind like "What is going to happen now? This happened out of nowhere. She didn't have any medical issues. How did this happen?" The next few days were a bit of a blur. I ended up staying the night with my grandmother and then the youth leaders until the funeral.

The day came for the viewing. There were flowers everywhere. There were so many flowers that they were even spread out all over the floor. My mom was only thirty-four years old. She left a husband, my two brothers, and me. I walked in to fix my mom's makeup and hair. I knew she would want to look pretty. So, I asked the funeral director when we picked the casket if I could get her ready and he agreed. As I fixed her hair and make-up, I placed my hand on hers. Her body was cold. I finished getting her ready and left to get dressed. When I returned to the funeral home, I placed the bell with the ice-skating girl in her casket. I looked at her as she was laying there, and thought of things she used to say to me. My mom's voice is prominent in my mind still. She would say: "If you can't buy me flowers when I'm alive, then don't buy me any when I'm dead." I was witnessing what she said she didn't want to happen.

The viewing started and hundreds of people poured into the funeral home. I was at the front door by myself. I greeted people as they came in, hugging them and thanking them for coming. People constantly told me how my mom would have given the shirt off her back to anyone. People whispered to each other saying, "Danielle isn't crying. Is she okay?" I could hear them. One of the women who had picked me up to go to church with her, approached me during the service and said, "Danielle, you doing okay?" I said, "Yes, I'm fine. I just keep telling people 'thank you for coming.'"

But I kept thinking to myself: where were all these people when my mom was alive?

After the funeral I stayed at the youth leader's house for a bit longer. The next week after the funeral, I was riding in the car with the youth leader's wife. We were driving to the saw mill to pick up checks to pay their employees. During the ride, she was talking about my mom's passing. She asked how I was feeling, and we chatted for a bit. Then, she asked me a question that changed the direction of my life from that moment forward.

She said, "I know this must be hard for you, honey. I can't imagine how you feel right now, but I have something to ask you."

You know those moments, when everything freezes? This was one of those once-in-a-life-time moments. I knew something was about to happen.

She continued: "My husband and I have been talking about you since your mom died. We know your dad works a lot. We also know he has a few problems, which you're well aware of. He will have to raise you and your brothers on his own." She continued, "Would you want to live with us full time?" I replied: "Wait. Really?" She said, "Yes. I am serious. My husband and I love you very much, and we would like to adopt you into our family." In that split moment, I thought so many things: "They don't fight. Their home is spotless. They are happy. I can learn so much from them, and, of course," my teenager mind thought: "I bet I will get cool clothes too!" I looked at her and responded "Yes! I can't tell you how much I love you both, and it would be a dream-come-true to be a part of your family." She said they would need to talk to my dad.

We met with my father the next day. They asked him if I could live with them, and if he would give them custody. He asked me if that is what I wanted. I said "Yes." He said, "Okay." And I walked into the house, grabbed a few of mother's things to keep for memories, packed my clothes and shoes. I took a moment to stand in the doorway of our home one last time. I didn't know if I would ever be back. Feelings of various emotions running through my body. I was excited, nervous, scared, sad, but also, I felt a sense of peace. A few days later we all met at the judge's office in Gate City, VA. My dad and the youth leaders were there with me. My dad signed full custody to the youth leaders.

I turned fifteen just two months after that.

I lost my mother, and yet now I had a new family and a new opportunity.

In Napoleon Hill's great book, *Think and Grow Rich* he wrote: "Every adversity, every failure, every heartache carries with it the seed of an equal or greater benefit." I believe that. Life is full of unfortunate circumstances that confront us. Still, everything happens in our life for a reason. The circumstances that unfold in our lives push us to overcome, become more, and create new break-throughs in progress. The only thing consistent in life is *change*. Adapting to change is the only way to succeed in life. There's that word again, "succeed:" the *progressive* realization of a worthy ideal.

I had no idea what was going to happen in my life when my mother passed away. I was just old enough to understand she wasn't going to be there to help me any longer. It felt like the rug had been pulled from under me. I felt confused, afraid, and defeated. But the opportunity to create a new life with my adopted family was a miracle. When your life brings your unfortunate situations, you may not know how they're going to turn into opportunities. Sometimes the most devastating scenarios turn into rewarding gains, and they happen faster than you expected. Other times, it's a slow process that happens over years, or even decades. In your daily life: turn stumbling blocks into stepping stones. Take everything that comes at you. Use it to get closer to your dreams. Your attitude during difficult situations will directly impact your outcomes. In order for you to thrive in life with the least amount of suffering, you must have the ability to transform adversity into action and opportunity. Be unassailable. Be solid in your conviction that everything always works out for the best.

There are seeds in adversity.

Chapter Four:

The Bridge to Your Future

"You cannot control what happens.
You can control how you respond."

In the few years that followed, our new family moved from Clinchport, Virginia, to Bristol, Tennessee. I was going to a different school. That was a blessing because no one knew about my mother's death in the new school. No one knew me at all. I did not have to worry about whether my schoolmates were laughing about my dad "giving me up." I was singing and playing music in church. I was even leading the worship at times. I spoke at a Woman's Conference on "Temperance."

When I met new people, if they asked about my family, I referred to them as my "Adoptive family."

My biological dad got remarried, and was diagnosed with Lou Gehrig's Disease. My Brothers were in and out of jail. However, my life had made a turn for the better. I believe that is directly related to the attitude I maintained. I constantly reminded myself that I cannot control the things that have happened in my life, but I can choose to never allow circumstances to reduce me, my self-worth, or my self-respect. My adoptive dad was a traveling evangelist. We had visited over twenty-five states. Some trips were for pleasure. Others were for his preaching engagements. When we travelled, sometimes I played music and helped in leading worship services. Life had really changed. My adoptive parents were such great influences. Sometimes, I still felt left out. When they bought things for their kids and forgot to buy me something, for instance. But I knew they didn't mean anything by it.

My adoptive dad got a call from a pastor in Seattle, Washington, one night. The pastor asked if my dad would come preach a revival for them. The pastor said he could pay for our family to fly there and stay at his home. I was so excited about the opportunity to visit a new state, and meet new people who were clearly sophisticated and successful. I was curious about wealthy people. What did they know that I didn't? If they can afford to pay for five people to fly, and pay my adoptive dad to preach, how did they do it?

The day arrived to go to the airport for our flight to Seattle. When we landed, the pastor picked us up, drove us to his house, and when we pulled up, it was huge! It was the biggest house I had ever seen. I thought to myself "Wow. Does he earn this much money preaching? If so: I want to be a preacher!" We walked in and he greeted us to his wife and two sons. The sons gave us a tour of their home: immaculate rooms, tall ceilings, and it even smelled clean, like perfume. One of the sons said, "I want to show you my favorite room!" He opened two large doors and there was a massive in-ground pool inside the house. I was in complete shock. That exists? I'd never even seen anything like that on TV. I kept my composure and I just kept thinking: "This is incredible. I need to get to know these people and learn what they do for work." Then, the other son said, "Oh if you like that room, wait until you see *my* favorite room. He walked us to the upstairs part of the house, showed us some bedrooms and bathrooms, and then he opened a door to a theater room. Oh my! Pinch me, please!? I felt like I was in a movie. I could not believe we were going to stay there all weekend. We got ready for our first night of revival.

We arrived at the church, and I played piano and performed sign language to one of the songs for the audience. My adoptive dad stood up in his suit and preached for the congregation. The next day the pastor took us on a "field trip" to a small airport. He drove us to a hanger – *his* hanger – and showed us his private plane. Not only that. We got in the plane and went on a flight tour of Seattle. With a curious and bewildered feeling, I thought to myself "What is this life?" The pastor was speaking through the microphone in the plane. He was pointing at all sorts of sights and telling us about Seattle. He pointed down and said, "See that little commercial section, right down there?" The plane tilted to the one side so we could see better. He continued, "That's one of the five Burger King locations we own." A wave of sadness ran through my body for a moment. Hearing about the pastor owning those four Burger Kings reminded me of the moment my adoptive mom got the call that my mother had died, which was just a few years prior. I hadn't thought about it in a while. Next: I recalled standing in that doorway in our home, day-dreaming about New York. As the moment passed, I heard the sound of my mom's voice in my mind: "You are exactly where you need to be, sweetheart." She used to tell me: "You never know who you're going to meet. Always be friendly and try to build relationships with anyone and everyone, because you never know who they are, what they do, how you may be able to contribute, or how they may help you."

The rest of the weekend we took time exploring Seattle. We went to Pikes Place, which was a bucket-list item for me. One of my favorite books is *Fish: A Proven Way to Boost Morale and Improve Results,* which is based on Pikes Place. When we got to the airport, I had a notebook in my purse so I could write on the plane ride back. When we got on the plane, I took my notebook out and began writing:

"I've learned so much this past week. I never thought I would experience something like this. I have traveled a lot. I have learned so much about life, people's careers, and their lives. When I get back home I need to apply for jobs. In order for me to achieve my hopes and dreams I need to start working as soon as possible."

I had been helping my adoptive family with their accounting, and miscellaneous tasks around their business, while focusing on school. When we return to Bristol, I applied to work for a bunch of different restaurants.

I got a call back, an interview, and then hired for my first job. My professional career was about to begin with the restaurant: Long John Silvers.

Chapter Five:

You're Worth More

"Your work ethic, dedication, and showing up determine your opportunities in life."

At nineteen years old, I looked back on my third year of working at the Long John Silver's restaurant chain. I had worked every area of the business: from opening, closing, preparing food and cooking, inventory, registers, drive-thru, cleaning, and everything in between. I maintained that job while I worked and completed a co-op position through school, working as a secretary for six months with an insurance company. The pastor's airport hangar stuck in my mind. I thought of it often. It motivated me to work hard. I was managing school, two jobs, and still living a personal life. Remaining consistent with Long John Silver's enabled me to build new relationships with various individuals who came into the restaurant.

Creating rapport with the regular LJS customers could have seemed insignificant. "They're just the customers," after all. However, I never saw it that way. Remember: you never know who you're going to meet. I kept that in mind, always. I made sure that even when I felt down, I did whatever it took to put on my game face and greet my next customer with enthusiasm. I genuinely loved my job there. I loved my co-workers, and enjoyed being a part of a team. I understood there was a hidden opportunity in meeting a new person on a daily basis. Treat that person as if they are the most important person in the world. In their mind, they *are.* I thought to myself: Either way, I believe a smile goes a long way. I think to myself: "Some of these people may be managers, executives, or business owners. Even if they're not, I'm going to treat everyone as if they are. Always leave a customer better than they were when they show up."

On that last point, I'd like to extend this to you. Sometimes our day-to-day experience can feel like were just "putting in time," and working strictly for a paycheck. I met countless people in those three years at

LJS who were ungrateful, indignant, and pessimistic about their job. They were constantly watching the clock. They put in the bare amount of effort. It seemed like their slogan for work was "do what's necessary to not get fired," instead of: "become more valuable and expand my opportunities." Those people did not approach their work as an opportunity. They treated it like they were victims of "*the system*," and that's exactly what they got. When you get the minimum *from* your work, it's because you're giving the minimum *to* your work. I always thought of work as more than a paycheck, no matter how trivial. It's always been a game. The better you get (regardless of pay) the more valuable you become. The better you get, the more valuable *you are.* At the end of the day, our character and work ethic shine through, and make us stand out. You, and your character become a bargaining chip you can use to advance yourself. You can make yourself more valuable. Ask yourself, "On a one to ten scale, do I approach my job 'all-in,' no matter how small or seemingly insignificant the task?"

Let's continue…

I knew there were hidden opportunities. Both in the connections with my coworkers and within our customers. Each moment *meant* something. Each job was paving the way for bigger things to come. That image of

New York was still consuming my mind. I knew the ultimate goal I wanted to accomplish. I knew my heart that every day was like placing one brick in a foundation.

One busy afternoon, a woman walked in who worked at the real estate company in the shopping center next door. I greeted her with a smile: "One baked cod meal, no butter, only rice, and no hushpuppies... on the way!" She was a regular and I had served her before. She said "Actually, I am not eating today. I came to talk with you." Surprised, I responded, "Oh, okay, what's going on?"

She said, "I have noticed your work ethic over the last several months." I felt flattered and acknowledged. She continued, "I've also overheard several of the real estate agents talking about 'that one server over at Long John Silver's with the positive energy.'" I said, "Well thank you. I love my customers and this is a really fun job." She said, "I can tell you love it. I noticed you never complain, and I've seen you in, what clearly is absolute chaos here when it's busy. Yet, you keep a positive attitude." I was probably blushing by then. She went on: "We're looking for a secretary in our office. If you're interested, you could work there during the day, and here at LJS at night. it would be a salaried position working eight to five. Is that something you would be interested in?"

Excited, I replied: "Yes, I would love to learn more about this." We continued our discussion and I accepted the job shortly after that conversation. Just a few short months later, I was promoted to a higher salaried position as a Client Care Manager running my very own Real Estate Office.

Your attitude towards your current career, opportunities and work, are either positive or negative. You can be grateful for what you have, or be a downer and whine about what you don't have. You can either see the glass half full or half empty. It is your choice. Being successful is not easy, but having the right attitude can be. Accomplishing bigger things is difficult to do. The reason is because it's a combination of smaller things that build up and compound over time. Most people do not focus on doing mundane work well enough, or to consistently high standards. Success requires lots of work, quick thinking, motivation, desire, and persistence. You must be mindful of your future desires and take control of your attitude. I could have chosen to feel as though my job was "just a job, and after all, I'm *only* working at a fast food restaurant." I did not look at it in that way, though. I chose to see that as an opportunity to learn how to run a scalable business. Perhaps that was due to the pastor in Seattle. He was not flipping the burgers. He was the owner. In order to get to that position, I learned you need to develop those exceptional customer service skills on the front line. I built relationships with regulars. I spoke to each coworker with respect. I put in real energy and effort to build my bigger dream.

If you think your work is "just a _____ job," than that is all it is going to be. If you think it is an opportunity to learn and grow, then you will learn and grow. What you put in your mind is what comes out in your activity. It comes out in your energy. You'll become what you train yourself to think. Instead of looking at work as if it is just a moving hand on a clock, look at every day as an opportunity to learn something different.

Ray Kroc, the founder of McDonald's, said, "Work is the meat in the hamburger of life."

When you go to work, say "good morning," and smile at your co-workers, employees, customers, or clients. Choose to be positive. I'm not talking "Pollyanna Positivity" where you're walking around with a fake smile, saying everything is nice. I'm talking about choosing to take affirmative action. When you say you're going to be ten minutes early, you do exactly that, and treat your word like gospel. When you hear that internal voice saying all sorts of negative stuff, you choose to point out three times the number of things that *are going well*. You suggest – no, *command* – your mind to focus where you want it to go. You may say…

- "Dear mind: focus on positive characteristic of [first name]."
- "Dear mind: in the next 3o seconds, think of moments you're appreciative for."
- "Dear mind: what lesson did we gain here?
- "Dear mind: how could we turn this situation into an advantage? List the ways we could do that right now."
- "Dear mind: thank you for solving all those challenges from the past where I persevered. We make a great team, and I appreciate you, always."

I know that may sound a bit strange to some people. But, listen, sometimes we need to play these mind-games with ourselves. These are like mental pushups, pullups, and squats. At first, they burn and you just want to give up. But, soon, you realize you've built up strength and can do more of them. The burn never goes away. You do, however, gain a comfort within that discomfort. Doing hard stuff makes hard stuff *easier*. Life is hard, and we need to do whatever it takes to achieve our hopes and dreams, suffer less, and refocus on what's important.

Do the challenging task. It teaches you that *YOU ARE WORTH MORE*.

Chapter Six:

Leaps of Faith

"You lose every risk you don't take."

A t twenty-two, I felt as though I had reached my maximum potential within my career as the secretary and then branch manager. My next step was becoming a real estate agent, but I wasn't ready to make that move at that point in time. So, I asked for a raise. My boss kindly replied that he could give me $0.35 more an hour. I was thankful, but I knew I could earn more. I also knew, as I had mentioned before about building up bargaining chips, that I had become more valuable. I opened the office every day. I was running the payroll. I was making the bank deposits and billing the agents for their monthly fees, in addition to running reports on their transactions with the printers, etc. I was basically running the company by myself, with fifteen of the top Real Estate Agents in the area to be accountable to. I decided to pick up a waitress job at a small mom-and-pop Italian restaurant located in the same shopping center as my real estate office. I thought to myself: "If I am not working, what else am I going to do?" I had the work ethic. And, honestly, I feared my former life creeping back in: being in the position my family had been in while I was growing up. I wanted to continually improve my lifestyle in the progressive realization of worthy pursuits. I was saving money every paycheck. Still, I came to the conclusion that I was stagnant. There was simply no way I could earn more. I had maxed out my time. It didn't seem like I could make the kind of money I wanted in order to live my ideal life. I remember being a little girl, seeing the BMW symbol, and thinking to myself how beautiful the car was and how I wanted to own a car like that. I remember riding in a Red Audi with a girlfriend in high school and telling myself I wanted to own one. There I was, sitting in my office, thinking about what my next leap of faith would be. I needed to do something different. I was making okay money, but not enough to own either one of those cars. I again, thought to myself,

"There has to be more to life than this." My days were turning habitual with no intellectual growth. I felt kept and domesticated and restless.

Mind Image: "Business suit. Tall building. New York."

I needed to come to terms with the situation. My goal was achievable, *potentially*. However, if I kept doing the same things every day in my life, and expecting different results, I was acting insane. I'd only achieve my goals if I took a bigger and bolder action.

Later that week, I visited a church family who lived in Anderson, SC. I loved visiting that place. I thought maybe I just need a change of scenery. So, I made a call and asked the family if I could visit them for the weekend. They agreed. Thursday afternoon, I packed my car and planned on staying for the weekend. Friday came. Thoughts ran through my mind: "Where am I going to live? How am I going to do this? I need a change. If I don't invest in myself, who will? If I don't take the risk and become better, how will I ever get there?"

I went to church weekly, living a very conservative and religious life. But again: "there has to be more to life than this." I was ecstatic about the trip; nervous, scared, anxious, and unsure of what I was really doing. I just knew I was taking a chance.

The drive to South Carolina is absolutely breathtaking. There are limitless views of the mountains and colors of the trees, radiating through the valleys. I made a pit-stop at an overlook in the mountains. As I stood there, my mind was racing. I didn't know how that life change was going to happen, yet knew it was up to me. I jumped back in the car and continued.

At one of my next stops at a restaurant, I asked the manager what she recommended to eat. I noticed she was practically doing everything by herself. We started talking. She explained how she lost some employees and was looking for a marketing manager. I continued inquiring about the business, and explained my experience with restaurants, and that I was a Client Care Manager of an office back in Tennessee. She replied "We are actually hiring. Would you like an application?". Something told me to say yes, so I did and then ordered lunch. While I waited for the food, I begin filling in the application. A bit later, she returned with the meal. I thanked her and handed her the application. When she returned to ask if I needed anything, I asked for a drink refill and the check. She returned with the drink in one hand, the receipt in the other hand, and some paperwork. I invited her to take a seat. She began asking me when I could start working. I replied I would like to wait at least a week, so I could take this move into serious consideration. She agreed and officially offered a job as a marketing manager for Sticky Fingers in downtown Greenville. I had already made my decision. I saw the opportunity and jumped on it. I took a Leap of faith to move to Greenville. I had a new job, and I had only been there for a day. I went out to dinner that night to celebrate!

While sitting at a bar, a tall-dark-and-handsome man walked in and sat beside me. We chatted a lot that night and he ended up asking me to come back the following weekend. I agreed. The next two weeks I was driving back and forth from Tennessee to South Carolina. I was learning how to live "out of my car" and hotel rooms as I prepared to move. I realized I had nowhere to live! I had been looking for apartments but I really wasn't sure what to look for. I knew the church people in case I needed to stay with them for a few days, but that was temporary. I also had money I had been saving. Still, I took the leap of faith and I moved to South Carolina. I was nervous. I was scared. Yet, I had one goal in mind. That was to take a chance and make a change. The only thing that is stopping you from changing is you. You have to get out of your comfort zone, and take calculated risks. Move toward your goals, even if, especially if, they scare you. You also must fail sometimes in order to succeed. I was told most of my life that if you make $40K per year, then you are living well. But I saw families struggle financially at that level; people who appeared complacent in their lives and scared of taking chances due to their fears. I have always thought that my biggest fear in life was failure. But I learned that with every failure I became stronger, more independent, and more resilient to life's uncertainties. Are you in a place in your life that is stagnant? Are you scared of taking a chance? Taking a Risk? What's stopping you? Are you aware your fears? You have to establish what is out of your comfort zone, and break through it. Don't settle for what you've had before. Get out of your comfort zone and take that next leap of faith. You will make it. Apply for that job you've been desiring. Ask that person on a date. Leave that negative person in the dust. Move. Do. Act. The only person stopping you from reaching your hopes and dreams is you, and you're also the only person who can do something about it.

Chapter Seven:

Pivotal Mind Change

"Get out of your comfort zone, take risks,

fail, fall, and figure out how to

pick yourself back up."

I put in my two-week's notice with the real estate company. I felt excited to move to South Carolina for my new job. I packed my car and travelled back and forth each weekend, staying in hotels. The relationship with Mr. Tall-Dark-Handsome was flourishing too. Within three weeks, I finally moved down there. Yet, I didn't plan well on the financial side. I was using the money I had saved from my jobs in Virginia and

Tennessee. I started working at Sticking Fingers as the Marketing Manager, doing the marketing and business development for three of their locations. I was eating out every meal with co-workers at night, staying in hotel rooms, buying new clothes, and I found myself only having fifty-two dollars to my name. I had spent all the money I had saved. I had at least another week before I received my first paycheck. So, I decided to make a call to a close family member. I asked them if they would lend me three-hundred dollars to tie me over. I told them I would pay them back 5o% when I got my first paycheck, and then the remaining balance when I received my next one. They replied, "No. I'm sorry we won't do that. We will not support your lifestyle."

Their response felt like a punch to the face. It was an unforgiving reality check that I am not entitled to anything, and that the consequences of my actions are mine, and mine alone to handle. That night, I ended up sleeping in my car in a hotel parking lot at Crown Plaza. Laying in my driver's seat with my clothes in the back and in my trunk, I had an honest conversation with myself.

"Even though this is not the way I planned my life to look, I am not giving up. I am going to put myself out there, meet new people, and work through this challenge.

Danielle: the only person you can absolutely depend on is you. No one is coming to save you. If it is to be: it's up to me. Period. So, you must succeed. You must push yourself beyond this, and transform it into something greater." Even though I couldn't reveal my situation to my coworkers, I had to be honest with *myself*. I was not in a good spot. I had been careless with my money. Coming to terms with that reality was hard. Yet, it was necessary. I would not settle for failure.

The next morning, I woke up and I used the lobby restroom to wash up. I used their outlets to fix my hair with a dryer and the sink to get the wrinkles out of my clothes. The next day, I went to work at Sticky Fingers. I knew if I could work as a server, asap, I could get tips and use those for immediate needs. I asked the manager if I could work as a server in addition to my current position as a Marketing Manager. She agreed and asked when I could start. I said (as nonchalantly as possible): "Today." That day, I spent my lunch break learning all the tech systems so I could quickly become a server. That night I slept in my car again. I never told anyone about my lack of financial stability. The next day I served during the lunch shift. I earned just enough money to get a hotel room that night. I opened a bank account when I receive my first paycheck, and I kissed that paycheck with my lips! "Thank you, thank you, thank you!" Appreciation is always good. ☺. I made the decision to start putting all of my paycheck in the bank as savings and only living on the tips that I received as server. That meant I had to make lots of sacrifices in order to become financially stable again. Being uncomfortable became comfortable. I still had to pay the bills, such as my car payment, cell phone bill, credit card bill (that I had maxed out), and necessities. Debt is daunting. Therefore, I strategized my attack on a regular basis, and got to work like a boss.

I ended up asking a co-worker at Sticky Fingers if anyone had a place to stay. From there, I bounced around from place to place, staying wherever I could. How could I have allowed myself to get to this point? "It is okay that I am not okay. But it's not okay for me to stay this way." I kept repeating. I knew those were important lessons to gain. I was learning. I was experiencing life. I was taking it in. I also made sure to never allow my circumstances to affect my career. I lived that way for quite some time; just getting by and saving as much money as I possibly could. I got my bank account up to $1,500 and finally secured an apartment. That is when my new chapter truly began.

How many times have you thought to yourself: "This isn't the way I planned my life."? How many times have you been irresponsible with your finances, and it cost you? You have to exchange complacency for productivity in order to achieve your goals. If you're going to procrastinate, then procrastinate *at procrastination*. Relax and chill, *tomorrow*. Get stuff done *NOW*. I could have chosen the security of living in Tennessee. I could have remained complacent. But I knew I was greater than what I *thought* I was. I desired more out of life. You have to make uncomfortable decisions in order to achieve greatness. If you've been going through the same routine day in and out just to be able to pay rent, then it's time to get mad at your current situation and do something *productive* about it. You must fight your Self to make your situation change. You must tell yourself "I am done. I am tired of being okay with how I am living my life now. It is my responsibility to own this situation." Show no love to apathy, laziness, and complacency.

If you feel disgusted, or ashamed, or bitter about your current life: good. Use those negative emotions to make changes. Set goals. You must have goals that will add purpose to your life. You are going to struggle. There is no other way. You are going to get knocked down. It's an almost absolute guarantee. You are going to feel pain. Yes. You're also going to get back up and try again. There will be a next day to act, again. You only get one chance at this life. You get one shot to live the way you want, but you have multiple chances each passing moment to redirect. Right now. Now, is the moment you've been waiting for. Write down your next objective. Write down your next move. Do it.

My irresponsible money management did not defeat me. I would not allow it to. I chose to see the positive. I was taking a risk in a new town, making investments in relationships. I know people who thought I was going to fail. I know people who were disappointed in me for trying, for moving, for striving. I know I had every reason to fail. The truth is, I didn't allow the situation to define my reality. If you stop worrying about what people think of you, and within that moment you take some form of big action, that's when you know you have chosen a different life. That's when you know you're on a new path.

Are you living this life the way you want?

Or...

Are you living your life for others?

What if you started living your life for you?

What would you do differently, right now?

Do that.

"Get uncomfortable to get comfortable."

"It is okay to not be okay.

It is not okay to stay that way."

Chapter Eight:

Know Your Worth

"Every NO is an opportunity for a YES."

It was Autumn. All afternoon I had been going to interviews. I finished my day by attending a pickup basketball game my husband was playing. (Yes, Mr. Tall-Dark-Handsome and I went all the way). I entered the field with a suit on. The referee, a friend of my husband's, asked why I was dressed up. I explained that I was looking for a new job opportunity. He told me the people at his wife's company were looking for help. I asked for her information. I reached out the following day. During the phone call, she expressed how they were looking for someone to help with software data entry.

She said it was a good job, with fair pay, but not a permanent one. That was okay with me. I advised her of my experience with accounting software. I told her I'd be happy to interview for the position and help out. We did the interview and I accepted the job. Shortly after, they had a company cookout. I had the opportunity to meet several of the employees. I introduced myself to a man who was very elegant in his appearance. As we were chatting, he explained that he was a retired partner of a CPA firm. We discussed my background of working in accounting, customer service, and sales, as well as running an office with agents back in Tennessee. Later that week, I received a follow-up call from him. He told me he was looking for someone to work for him as an executive assistant. He wanted someone to help manage company budgets, customer service, sales, and accounting. He told me to think about it and email him if interested. I sent an email of appreciation for his call. He replied and we established a time to interview. He officially offered the job to work for him. I worked for him for about eight months. During those months I had saved the company a bunch of money, finding errors in accounts payable. I was wearing many hats again: managing the customer service department, acting as HR manager, assisting sales with trade shows, managing budgets for this company and assisting with managing budgets for other entities he was a vice president for.

I wanted a raise. I had saved the company a lot of money, and it was clear to me by now, that these skillsets had become habit. I could identify my value. I understood that, without me, certain losses would have continued occurring (which were many multiples more than my salary). While speaking to a coworker and friend about that, she encouraged me to simply ask for a raise. She said, "If you don't ask for it, then you certainly won't get one." I thought to myself: she is absolutely right! So, I sent my manager an email asking for a meeting. We scheduled it and the day had soon arrived.

His office was cold, with walls chock full of degrees and awards. We started the conversation as any other, casually talking. Then I pulled out a few pieces of paper I had prepared. The pieces of paper revealed all the different ways I had helped save the company money. I proceeded to sell myself. Then, I asked the tough question:

"Can I have a raise?"

I felt anxiety, and was so nervous. Yet, I had reviewed my own performance. I was confident I deserved that raise. He looked at me and said:

"No."

It took every ounce of my courage to reply:

"I don't understand. Why not?"

He responded:

"You do not have a college degree."

Again, I had to dig way down. It was either *keep cool,* or *show emotions and cry*, which would mean I wasn't managing my emotions.

"I understand that. However, a college degree shouldn't determine if I receive a raise or not. My work performance should determine my raise."

He replied, "I am not giving you a raise. That's my final decision."

I felt so rejected, disappointed, sad, and angry. I thought back to when I was sleeping in my car in that hotel parking lot. I didn't sulk or argue when my family would not lend me $3oo. I didn't feel entitled to it. They owed me nothing, and all I could do was ask. But this was not fair. I had *earned* a raise. Still, I remained calm and composed. I did not show any emotion. I smiled and said, "I understand, thank you for your time" and left the office. I returned to my desk, where I had a quote posted in my cubicle wall that said: "Every NO is an opportunity for a YES." That's my degree. It's a degree I earned from my years in the University of Hard Knocks. That night, I gave myself a raise. I raised my chin up. Then said,

"Danielle, you are your own advocate for success, and I'm hiring you to maximize my value!"

(Hustle Mode: Engage).

I started checking different job websites.

I applied for whichever positions seemed interesting.

I went to my professional network and put out some feelers for opportunities.

I responded to various recruiters and personal contacts who had been trying to recruit me.

Within just a few weeks I was offered a job making 25% more money, with more responsibilities. I knew this next position would enable me to grow more, learn more, and become more. I took the opportunity.

Our success in life is determined by our responses to rejection. We can either allow rejection to defeat us, or motivate us. Failure is not an option. I was not going to sit back and allow my manager to determine my worth. I knew what I had to offer. I saw the numbers. I knew that I was worth more and didn't allow his lack of validation to stop me from earning what I was worth. I could have accepted his statement, went back to my desk and continued working, feeling uncertain about the amount of money I was earning. I could have accepted his views of me. However, I understood my college status did not define my work experience, work ethic, ambition, and dedication to achieving goals. Whether they be my goals or the strategic objectives of the companies I work with, name the *result* and I'm getting it. You can develop that mindset too. Everyone experiences rejection. Life is full of bewilderment with a roller coaster of emotional stress. No matter what you're going through right now, or have gone through in the past, know that your attitude is your choice. Life is ten percent what happens to you, and ninety percent how you respond to it. Your life is like an art canvas. You get the opportunity to paint your own picture every day. If you don't like where you are right now, start on a new canvas until you paint your masterpiece. It is never too late to start over. Live your life with intention. Believe in yourself. Don't allow anyone to define you by your mistakes or circumstances. Know your worth.

"Life is ten percent what happens to you and ninety percent how you react to it"

"Know Your Worth."

Chapter Nine:

Circumstances Aren't *You*

"We either make ourselves miserable
or we make ourselves strong,
the amount of energy is the same."

I was working for a company that was in the process of promoting me to manage larger accounts. I was leading sales for the company. My husband and I were expecting our first child. I was traveling for work, teaching Zumba and RIPPED fitness classes at a gym in downtown Greenville in addition to my Sales and Business Development career. I was married to my dream man, seven-months pregnant, had raised myself out of poverty all by myself, and was feeling very proud of my progress. By that point, I had earned enough to buy the car I saw as a child in the church parking lot: a beautiful BMW.

I wanted to get a whole bunch of traveling done before our baby arrived, so I made plans to go to a casino with some friends. We had a great time. I returned from the casino; my husband was sleeping with his phone beside his head in our room. I picked it up to place it on the charger and saw messages between he and another girl. My husband was cheating on me. "I'm seven months pregnant and my husband is cheating on me." One of my biggest fears is being a single mother and that was happening.

I confronted him. Yet, the conversation was futile. He had broken my trust, and it was unforgivable. Having said that, at the time I didn't know what to do. So, I rationalized his poor behavior, and tried giving him the benefit of the doubt. In other words, I tolerated his disrespect, which in turn *enabled* more behavior. I ignored my feelings about it. I stuffed them down into some hidden place, and tried as best I could to move forward.

The following Monday, I went to work. I did not tell my boss, co-workers, or even my closest of friends what was going on. I continued working as if nothing happened. I was dealing with the possibility of a divorce. My heart was broken, and I didn't know how I should attempt to forgive him and work through it as our marriage vows stated. Again: "For better or for worse." It was feeling like our marriage was for worse.

I bottled everything in. Time was passing. I continued catching my husband in lies. I was working lots of hours, trying to make sure I stayed focused, all the while feeling fears of being a single mom and fighting the head trash of not feeling worthy, respected, or loved. I was trying to avoid those feelings from affecting my work. My new position required me to travel to California monthly. I was choosing to maintain a positive attitude at work. I was trying to be excited about this little person I was about to meet.

Our baby was born. I stayed at the hospital. My husband's family were there with me, and my husband went back and forth to his office. I was feeling rejection and alone. I continued choosing to believe that everything would work out for the best. Those mental conversations required digging really deep within my spirit to find raw material I could use as motivation. It took every ounce of courage, as it had each and every time before that. Nevertheless, I traversed through the battle-field of emotion, chin up, never sulking.

My company's annual awards ceremony happened to be in Greenville, South Carolina, that year. Aiden, my son, was two weeks old. My friend drove me to the awards ceremony. My husband stayed home with Aiden. During the ceremony I received "Sales Excellence: Highest Gross Profit in the Organization" Award. I was astounded, excited, and feeling proud of myself for accomplishing such an award while going through pregnancy and dealing with the revelation of my husband's affair. Fast-forward two months, and I was pursued by a software company. I explained to them that I had very little experience in selling software, however, I would do whatever it took to learn it and sell it. Seven interviews later (yes: seven!), I was offered and then accepted the job.

My husband and I officially went through a divorce. The poem my mom wrote before she passed away resonates in my mind: "Dear Mr. Right. You came into my life and I became your wife. You took me for granted as I held my hand out to you, it was my love that was always true. But you'll wake up someday and I'll have gone astray out finding someone who can love me for who I am today. You should have loved me for who I was, giving me kisses and lots of hugs. But now you're crying over me and I'm happy and free to be me who you couldn't see." That summarizes my reality in that moment.

The positive side was that I started a new job! I'm not letting anyone take me down. As I said earlier: *Hustle Mode: Engage!* I was living with my best friend (for the time, at least, while I was transitioning from my marriage). I returned to teaching Zumba and RIPPED classes. I was a single mom with primary custody. I kept pushing forward, never allowing my circumstances to prevent me from progressing. I thought to myself: "There has to be more to life than this" and continued balancing whatever life was throwing at me. Within the first four months in my new position as an Account Manager and Pre-Sales EAM Consultant, I had received an award for "5 Net New Wins in Q3" and "14 Net New Wins Year to date". Those were two accomplishments that no other sales individual had achieved in the company before. All that pain in my personal life was not going to be an excuse for becoming complacent.

Problems pledge allegiance to no one. Regardless of gender, color, political viewpoint, or nationality, you will always have some sort of challenge arise in your life. Problems are something we all share. No one has ever been granted immunity from them. They are always going to enter our lives. It's our choice whether we want to allow those problems to make us suffer. Our life plans are never going to play out exactly as we envision them. That's one of the beautiful parts of life. We can never anticipate which problems we are going to encounter, or when. Life is what you make of it. Determined individuals handle their problems.

They say to themselves:

1. This is what is real right now: a., b., c., and d.
2. Here's what I am going to do to solve it: first... then... next... then...

... and they go for it.

Your response to your problems determines your success. Your circumstances do not determine who you are. We either make ourselves miserable or we make ourselves strong. The amount of energy is the same. Wherever you are in your life, choose to see all the positive aspects. Choose to face your problems head on. Handle them carefully, being intentional and methodical. Being optimistic doesn't mean you try to force negative situations to be less painful. That's resistance. Being optimistic means: finding positivity in every situation. It's directing your focus. Despite how bad some of the life situations were, having optimistic thoughts allowed me to persevere through the adversities I faced. They made me stronger. Your challenges can make you stronger too. I was able to look past my situation and remain focused on my goals and dreams.

NEVER let go of your dreams.

Circumstances are not YOU.

Chapter Ten:

Be a Leader

"Be audacious, aggressive,
and enthusiastic."

Working for the EAM Software company, something new unfolded out of the blue. They were suddenly acquired by another company. We had no idea it was going to happen, and it was quite a surprise. The office had fear, anxiety, and tension floating around like a smog. Lots of chatter was going on about what was going to happen next. Who is going to get let go? Although the management team was trying to clear the ambiguity, it was still prevalent. We were advised the executive team was going to visit us over the following weeks. I proactively researched all of the team members who were going to come to our office. I researched their names, their employment history, and what they look like. I my had career goals in mind, and I was strategizing how to communicate my value to anyone who would interview me. I was on the right track to success.

The day came. The executive team was planning to meet and speak with our team. I took a quick break and ran to the restroom before our anticipated meeting. As I departed the restroom, in walks the CEO of the company that acquired us. I immediately recognize her.

I called her by name: "Hi, it's nice to meet you, Kim. I'm Danielle. We're excited to see what you're going to do with our company."

As I mentioned before, I had done all sorts of research on their company. I wanted to be proactive with this transition and have the highest possibility working with the company that had acquired us. So, I was genuinely excited. She looked at me with surprise, and responded, "Hi, it's nice to meet you, too. Thank you." I said, "You're welcome. I will see you in the office"

The next few weeks were even more ambiguous. Employees were being let go of left, right, and center. Management was scrambling, trying to keep everyone calm. Most of the employees I was surrounded with were being let go. I was one of the few that was making it past the job cuts. On a Monday morning, I was advised that I would be meeting the Regional Vice President of Sales later that week. He was visiting from Atlanta. I was excited to no end. I was eager to see the outcome of that meeting.

The day came. The meeting was in just a few minutes. I was dressed to impress; full business pant suit, closed toe shoes, hair done, light jewelry, and light perfume. The time was getting closer and closer for us to meet. I was getting nervous but still also excited. I looked over at my wall that is filled with quotes and personal goals. I whispered to myself: "I am ready for this meeting. I've done all the research. This is a critical moment that's going to help me achieve all those goals on that wall." A co-worker came to me and said, "He's ready to see you." I had a current, updated resume in hand. I had no clue what the meeting was going to be about. All I knew was that I felt like I needed to sell myself.

I walked into the room, looked at him in the eyes, and greeted him with a solid handshake. We sat down. He began asking me about me. He asked "interview type" questions. Then, he asked me three questions that ended up resulting in a completely new direction in life.

He said, "What do you want to do for your career?" Then, "What makes you happy?" and then, "What are your career goals?" I responded by telling him my desire was to be in management, that I'm a great leader and coach, and that I believe I am destined for more than what I am. I explained my love to help people, and seeing them become the best version of themselves. I shared how my desire is to help people see the potential in themselves, and that I understand how people can't see it until they have someone to reflect it back to them. He then asked questions regarding my resume. He asked me why I didn't obtain a bachelor's degree. I replied that I had a choice to either work or go to school, and I chose to work. I explained my experience in various departments and my eagerness to learn and willingness to be challenged, and do whatever I could do to improve my performance for the company, and make a successful life for my son and me.

Then he asked more questions I'd never been asked in an interview

"What is your biggest fear?"

"My biggest fear is failure."

"What do you feel like your biggest failure was?"

"I feel like my biggest failure was my divorce."

He said, "Why do you feel it was your biggest failure? Was it your decision?"

"My husband made decisions that led me to file for divorce. There was nothing I could do to make the marriage work. No matter how much I seemed to forgive him, he kept lying about his behavior, and I do not tolerate people who steal, cheat, or lie. That also led me to facing my other biggest fear, which was being a single parent."

I then said, "I am a happy, positive, and upbeat person. I know that I deserve someone who loves me for me, who respects me the way I respect them. I want my son to grow up seeing the happy mom I truly am. I want him to grow up understanding that we have to be responsible for our actions and that there are consequences for the choices we make. I also want him to know that in life we have to make difficult decisions in order to better ourselves."

He stopped me and replied, "I can tell you are a very strong woman. Very determined. You have respect for yourself, and that self-respect caused you to face two of your biggest fears. You chose the difficult road, taking on challenges and not only facing them, but owning them, and becoming a better person for it."

He proceeded to say he had heard of my accomplishments during my employment with the company his just acquired. We finished the conversation. This was the longest meeting anyone else had been given. Later that day, I began to draft a "thank you" email to him. I explained I would be interested in the opportunities his company offered that would be a good fit. He replied the next day. We scheduled a follow-up meeting for the following week. We had the meeting. He told me about a Solutions Consultant position that his company was in need of. This individual would be responsible to demonstrate the financials of an ERP Software (Enterprise Resource Planning). I was later asked to go to Atlanta and meet with others from that division of the company. They advised that I'd have three weeks to learn the software. After those three weeks I would come back and perform a demonstration of the software to individuals in the accounting department, along with other executives.

I returned, passed the test, and was offered the job as an Enterprise Solutions Consultant. I was traveling and learning more and more about myself, the world, and corporate America. Due to his leadership and desire to see the best in his employees, he gave me an opportunity. It was up to me whether or not I would maximize that opportunity. But his leadership gave me that chance. He listened to me during the interview. He asked uncomfortable questions to get to know what my career goals and desires were.

In the competitive job market, I realized that everyone has to sell themselves to somebody. If you want a better job, you have to sell your experience to your boss and ask for more responsibilities. You have to explain why you are the right person for the job. That explanation is not a one-way street. It's a conversation. You're not *telling* them: you're *selling* them. You have to be audacious, aggressive, and enthusiastic. Best of all, you have to believe in yourself and what you are doing. That is the key to success in a job-market. Of course, that's if you've got the skills and work ethic, which we've already covered, previously. If you don't believe in yourself or what you're selling, people will see right through you. In order to be a leader, you must listen. Not only to respond, but to truly understand the other person's wants, needs, and desires. That leader relied on his instincts and intuition to see my desire to maximize the opportunity ahead. He wanted to see me become more than what I was, and step up to the promotion.

Being a leader means you're ready to take the lead no matter how difficult it might seem. Followers avoid not only taking risk but anything they would find challenging. I was proactive. I knew exactly what I wanted, and earned the right to ask for it. I knew I would have to put in extra effort and show leadership in order for me to be acknowledged as the right choice.

Be a leader. Start by leading yourself.

"We are our own product.

So, sell it like crazy."

Chapter Eleven:

Dreams Come True,

If You Have One

"Setting goals gives you something to strive toward and keeps you accountable to your word."

While working as an Enterprise Solutions Consultant for the software company, I was traveling weekly and bi-weekly. I genuinely loved it. I was finally earning six figures. I was constantly challenged beyond my abilities. I was pushed harder than I ever had been before: intellectually, professionally, and personally.

I accepted responsibilities beyond my current position. We learned of a new opportunity for a large manufacturing company that was considering merging with another organization. We went onsite to their plant in Cumming, GA. We performed our plant tours in addition to asking all sorts of discovery questions to determine what software solutions to suggest. We returned to the office and discussed the various solutions we felt may fit their needs. A few weeks went by and their team asked us to come to Chicago and share what solutions would be best to optimize the efficiencies within various other departments in their organization. In other words, our discovery session made an enormous impact on how they viewed our company.

The day arrived for us to head to Chicago. I was so excited and ecstatic to be going to the corporate office of this prestigious company to present our solutions for implementation. As we arrived in Chicago, I was so happy to mark travelling there off my bucket-list of places to visit. The next morning, I woke up eager to see how that day would go. I fixed my hair with curls, put my make up on, and brushed my teeth. I had music playing in the background, and then I put on my blue business suit. Ready to rock n' roll. I headed down to meet the others in the lobby. We all greeted each other and then discussed the presentation we were about to deliver.

We arrived at the corporate office building. As I walked up to the front door, my reflection was bold in the glass. I thought: "You go, girl." We walked in to speak with the desk concierge, who advised us we had to go through another security access point in order to arrive at our planned destination which was the 86th floor. Eighty-six floors! This place was huge. We arrived at our first stop: the 41st floor. We went through the security access point. This is big business. We all walked through, and got on the elevator to take us to the 86th floor. I was getting nervous. I had my laptop bag in one hand, and the other hand was placed in my suit pants pocket. We arrived: level 86. Ding! I walked into the room filled with CEO's, CFO's, and various other executives. I greeted everyone that was in the room and greeted the others as they entered. My heart is racing. I feel so lucky to even be in this room with such individuals. However; I am here. I think to myself "This is crazy". There was a moment of silence as people were getting their coffee and catching up on emails. I walked toward the window to admire the view.

As I looked around, my heart is racing and my mind went back to being the eleven-year-old girl with a dream:

a dream of being "successful" in a business suit in a tall building in New York. I think to myself in that moment "I made it. I really made it" So many emotions are running through my body. Feelings of wanting to cry from happiness, feelings of wanting to call a parent and tell them about my success. However; I keep my composure and I return to greeting others that entered the room. I realized in that moment: that although, this was not the New York tall building I had envisioned as an eleven-year-old girl: *that my dream had come true.*

My dream as an eleven-year-old girl finally came to fruition because I never stopped pursuing it.

- I was…
- Brought up poor
- Lived in trailer parks, in homes infested with roaches
- Was sexually abused

- Given up for adoption

- Homeless

- Divorced

- A single mother

- Felt unheard, unwanted, and unloved

... And still worked harder than anyone I knew to produce the vision of myself I held in my mind's eye. Constantly striving, I maintained that singular dream in mind. And there I was: looking out that window. I grabbed my phone and captured a picture of the Chicago sky rises *(See the image on the back of the book)* as a reminder that we really can be anything we want to be if we just put our minds to it. The meeting started and we talked, presented, strategized, and provided solutions that would help the company optimize their efficiency. We departed the office building, and headed toward the airport. Feeling accomplished, motivated, and more ambition than I had ever felt before: it was limitless. I had finally "made it." Our company continued to work with multi-million-dollar companies like the one I had presented to. Our job was to go onsite to those Fortune 500 companies and help them determine which software solution was right for them. Additionally, our goal was to coach them on implementation best practices and new business processes their companies needed in order to accomplish their business goals. I was traveling a lot, and missing time away from home with my son, yet feeling the most freedom I have ever felt.

I ended up being recruited into a real estate company and became the Vice President of Business Development. After a few weeks of negotiation, I accepted my first corporate Executive Role and I purchase another one of my bucket-list items: A red Audi. I had turned my life around. I was able to give my BMW away to someone who needed it. That was my first bucket-list item I wanted, and I was able to give it to a friend at no cost to them, including covering insurance for them for an additional six months; all because I *wanted* to. Just as my friend in school would buy me snacks and I told myself one day I want to be able to buy snacks for someone else. This wasn't a snack, but that is exactly how I felt as I watch them drive the car away. That felt so good.

Chapter Twelve:

Your Life, Your Career,

Your Choice

"We either create opportunities or we create excuses. The energy is the same."

Being a Vice President of Business Development, I enjoy wearing suits every day. I enjoy working with C level executives. I love working with various companies within the upstate. These were *my* missions in life. What are yours? Accomplishing my goals does not mean "the end." There is no end: success is a progression. Yet, I've finally turned myself into an example: someone who worked against odds to produce her dream. I believe it is possible for you, too.

Being alive is full of bewilderment sometimes. At the time of writing this, our world was recently hit with the Covid-19 crisis. Like most people, I am placed on Furlough (temporary leave). But unlike most people, I decided I am going… *Hustle Mode: Engage…*

… writing and publishing this book, while closing a deal and becoming the proud new Co-Owner of Gizmo Gastro Bar and Lounge in Downtown Greenville, and (the most important) spending a ton of quality time with my son.

Whenever there is complexity; there is opportunity. No matter how strange a moment in time can get, no matter how hard, no matter how challenging; opportunities exist. It's up to you to keep pushing forward. That skill was not granted to me. I developed it, using the mindsets I shared in this book. We either create opportunities or we create excuses, the energy is the same. Additionally, I started helping small businesses with their business operations. I was utilizing my experience as a solutions consultant for fortune 500 companies to help them scale their business and enable them to grow and expand their profits. Who would have ever thought that my dream when I was an eleven-year-old girl could come true?

Vision, dreaming, and a strong determination will enable you to achieve the desires you want for yourself. All my eleven-year-old self ever wanted was to be a successful businesswoman, in a suit, in a tall building, looking out over the city. That was all I desired. I didn't know how hard it would be to get there. At the same time, I did not want to live the same life I saw my parents living. I never would have dreamed all the "how" could possibly arrange in this way: no college degree, yet still managing a team in corporate America... Earning well over six figures, while raising my son as a single mother, after growing up in and out of trailer parks... Start and running my own real estate company... Achieving my dream of owning that BMW, and then an Audi, and been so financially stable that I was able to give the BMW away 100%.

I tell you all of this to confirm: no matter who you are, where you are in your life, where you are in your education, where you are in your career – you can be anything you want. "Our life," as the Roman emperor Marcus Aurelius said, "is what our thoughts make of it."

You have to be hungry to learn, passionate about your work, open to challenges, driven for success, open to failures, and willing to stretch yourself in order to grow. You have to pick yourself up every time you fail, and learn how to separate your personal life from your professional life. Don't take your personal life to work with you.

Listen to the people around you. Remember that people don't care what you know, until they know how much you care. It is so important to be patient, persistent, and persevere.

Also, you can't choose your family, yet you can create your social groups. Surround yourself with like-minded people. I realized that I needed to surround myself with people who supported my goals, dreams, and ambitions. I surround myself with people who believe in me, who I support 100%. These individuals motivate me and believe in me beyond my own vision of what's possible. Surround yourself with individuals who believe in you, when you cannot believe in yourself. You also need to be that person to others. Be someone that you would want to be friends with. Be someone you would want to date, marry, or work for. If you were your own boss, how would you rate your performance? If you were your own partner how would you rate yourself in that respect? Are you being the person you would want to come home to? Are you being the person you would want to work with? I surround myself with people who not only make me happy, but who uplift me, believe in me, and make me laugh when I am in need. Surround yourself with people who never take advantage of you; people who genuinely care about you. Those individuals are the ones worth keeping in your life. Everyone else is just passing through.

In life and your career, a lot of times you are going to experience reasons to fail, reasons to quit, and reasons to give up. Ask yourself if you have given everything you have to succeed.

My favorite quote of all time is by Michael Jordan, who said:

"I've missed more than 9000 shots in my career. I've lost almost 300 games. 26 times, I've been trusted to take the game winning shot and missed. I've failed over and over and over again in my life. And that is why I succeed."

Being someone who grew up playing basketball and loving the game, I have consistently placed this quote on my office walls, in my homes, and on social media. The question you need to ask yourself is: are you giving everything you can to reach your goals? Are you putting in the effort it takes to be who you really want? Are you living your life with intention?

The truth is: You are not going to achieve your goals and dreams by blaming circumstances. If you're not winning, it is not your parent's fault. If you're not winning, it's not your friend's fault. If you're not winning, it's not your partner's fault. It is you. It is your responsibility. If you've not reached your financial goals and dreams, it is because you have not taken the calculated risk to achieve your ambitions. Or, you have not put in the *correct* time, effort, energy, or work to get where you need to be. Why not? You need to ask yourself that: "why not?" Then, take absolute responsibility for the answer. Then take 100% control of the actions to correct your situation. I had every reason to fail, I had every reason to give up, I had every reason to stay complacent earning the $30K' I was making in Tennessee. Yet, I took chances, risks, and I put myself in uncomfortable situations in an effort to push forward. I persevered and you can too. I realized that my current situation was not going to get me where I wanted to be, so I took chances. If you allow your past to interfere with your present, you will never reach your goals and your dreams. That's it.

You need to establish what your goals, dreams, and desires are. Make your plan. Every day is a new day for opportunity. You are going to have pitfalls. They are inevitable. Pick yourself back up, wipe off your knees, and don't whine about it. Keep pushing forward. You are the only person stopping you from achieving what you want. Your attitude will either move you forward or backward, but your mindfulness of your attitude is your choice. Attitude is a small thing that makes a big difference.

Never give up.

Tenacity is in every cell of your being.

You have invaluable strength to keep moving toward whatever you want. This is despite your circumstances. Your persistence can overcome anything, and keeps you succeeding.

Live your life with purpose and intention; the life you have always dreamed of and imagined living.

It is the perfect time to be whoever you want to be.

There's no limit.

You can change or stay the same: you make your own rules. We can make the best or the worst of our lives. I hope you make the best of it. I hope you see things that startle you into action, feel things you've never felt before, and I hope you meet people with a different point of view. I hope you live a life you're proud of, and if you're not: I hope you have the strength to start all over again.

This is *your life.*

It's *your career.*

It's *your choice.*

Thank you!

Acknowledgments:

Thank you to my son, Thomas Aiden Britt IV for continually challenging me, which helped me write this book. No matter where life takes me, this book will always be a reminder of who your mom is, who she strives to be, and I hope it teaches you to contribute to society, be the best employee, friend, and leader one day. To never give up or stop pursuing your hopes and dreams.

Thanks to my co-worker who became my best friend, Holly Kennedy. Thank you for seeing my work ethic, encouraging me to continue pursuing my professional goals and dreams. Chris Kennedy, thank you for not only being the incredible husband you are to Holly, but for believing in me with all of my crazy career ideas, including writing this book. Thank you both for always reminding me of what I have accomplished in order to lift me up when I doubted myself. To my friend Kelly

Moore, thank you for standing by me when life continued to throw obstacles in my direction. Thank you for listening to me, providing humor, and providing edits for this book. Your friendship has been unassailable, and I can't thank you enough. Krista Maria, thank you for your passion for being a child advocate and giving people a voice who don't have one. Thank you for being another editor for this book, too. Each of your friendships of endless generosity, time, and supportive nights have made my life feel so much more fulfilling.

I am thankful to every boss who didn't give me the chance for a promotion, too. Thanks to every leader who took their job seriously, and invested in me. Thankful to every C level executive that I have met who has empowered me.

Huge thank you to Michael Byars, Marlon Hunter and Rich Haggins. You men deserve appreciation for your belief in my book dreams. Thank you for being there along the way as I drafted, composed, and wrote this book.

Sincere thank you to Shaun P Robertson (Co-Owner Gizmo Gastro Bar and Technical Repair lounge) for believing in me and partnering on Gizmo together.

A huge and special thank you to Colin Campbell from Formula Publisher, my editor and writing coach. Thank you for your patience with me while I re-wrote this book three different times! Thank you for believing in my creation and helping me bring it to light. I cannot wait to see how my career story encourages, empowers, and enables people to live better. Also, Brian Knox, thank you for the wonderful picture for the front cover. I appreciate your skill, your effort, and revisions, working with me to get the right image.

Thank you to each and every person who has chosen to be a part of my life and has loved me despite my energetic, optimistic, positive, forward thinking, personality.

I appreciate you.

About the Author

Danielle Britt, is a highly sought-after business operations expert, consultant, and advisor to C-Suite executives. She ascended the corporate world as a single mother of her son, Aiden. She now shares leaderships strategies for increasing performance, teamwork, confidence, and success in the corporate environment.

Made in the USA
Columbia, SC
13 July 2020